# The Healing Power of God

Begin Healing the Hurts of Your Past
and Open the Door to a Joyful Life

*by*
*Malcolm Smith*

**HARRISON HOUSE**
Tulsa, Oklahoma

06 05 04 03     10 9 8 7 6 5 4 3 2 1

*The Healing Heart of God*
*Begin Healing the Hurts of Your Past and*
*Open the Door to a Joyful Life*
ISBN 1-57794-611-1
(Formerly ISBN 1-88008-921-1)
Copyright © 2003 by Malcolm Smith
7986 Mainland Drive
San Antonio, Texas 78250
www.malcolmsmith.org

Published by Harrison House, Inc.
P.O. Box 35035
Tulsa, Oklahoma 74153

# Table of Contents

# Chapter 1

## The Key to Joy

The revelation that Jesus is the healer of our broken hearts is sadly missing in the lives of many believers. They have been well taught that salvation is the crisis that wipes out their past as if it never happened—a crisis that now gives them the strength to struggle to be like Jesus.

When struggling to be like Jesus doesn't "work," they feel there is something wrong with their salvation. Consequently, they go forward and accept Christ one more time; or they rededicate their lives to Him again and again, each time with the hope that maybe they will get it right this time!

> The Spirit of the Lord God is upon me, because the Lord has anointed me to bring good news to the afflicted; He has sent me to bind up the brokenhearted, to proclaim liberty to captives, and freedom to prisoners.
>
> Isaiah 61:1

This verse contains Jesus' job description! It is also the same verse that He read in the synagogue when He proclaimed that He was the Messiah. (Luke 4:18,19.)

Among other things, He is to "bind up the brokenhearted." Jesus is the One who heals broken hearts and brings joy to those who live in grief and despair.

## Unfulfilled Christianity

Many Christians find it next to impossible to have mature relationships with other people. If they are married, they are continually frustrated. They are unable to truly love their spouse because they cannot give themselves fully to another person. They don't know how to have open and honest communication or how to be good friends. At times, they wonder if they even know what love is.

Others have unresolved conflicts that extend back to their childhood. They are held in bondage to their past because they have failed to forgive those who have abused them. Or, they have abused others and have reached the conclusion they are unworthy of anyone's love and respect.

Still, other brokenhearted children of God are tremendously confused about who God is and where they fit into His picture. Most of them question whether they fit in at all!

I meet them in every service. They join in the worship and enthusiastically respond to the proclamation of the Word. If an altar call is given for salvation or rededication, they are the first to respond. However, when they leave the service, the sense of God's presence also seems to leave them. Downcast and depressed, they return to the bleak, gray world of their home and work.

Eventually, with a desperate yearning in their hearts, they cry out, "Isn't there more to Christianity than this? Is the presence of God only felt in the gathering of believers? Is my time of worship in church the only time I will experience joy in my life? The rest of the week seems so pointless and meaningless!"

Although they have accepted Christ as their Lord and Savior and have experienced the infilling of the Holy Spirit, many children of God have never been taught how to apply the Word of God to their everyday lives. The tragic result is that even though they are assured of eternal life, they live in misery and bondage all the way there! They sing of going to heaven when they die, but they have no song of rejoicing for the present!

## Salvation Is Ongoing

Accepting Jesus as our Lord and Savior comes from a crisis that begins a process, a process in which our broken hearts are healed and where we discover our new identity in Christ. We must be taught to live, not from ourselves, but from the Spirit of God who lives within us.

This process is referred to many times in the Old Testament, as the prophets anticipated the coming Messiah and His salvation. Malachi 4:2 describes the experience of salvation:

> But for you who fear My name the sun of righteousness will rise with healing in its wings; and you will go forth and skip about like calves from the stall.

In vivid imagery, the prophet calls Jesus the rising sun bursting into the darkness of mankind's living death. In His rays we would be healed. The believer is described as a calf coming out of the darkness of the stall into the sunlight, leaping and skipping about for the sheer joy of a whole, completely healed life. The Holy Spirit identifies Jesus with this prophecy in Luke 1:78-79:

> ...the tender mercy of our God, with which the Sunrise from on high shall visit

us, to shine upon those who sit in darkness and the shadow of death.

Many believers still sit in the shadow of death even though they are partaking of eternal life and are no longer dead. They need to be taught how they can rise out of their darkness and confusion, for their Light has come. (Isa. 60:1.) In fact, their lives can radiate His light to the dark world around them, like the calf who leaps for joy.

## What's in a Name?

Malachi 4:2 not only describes the salvation experience but also answers the question of how to heal a broken heart. Healing rays are said to come to those who "fear His name." This expression is not readily understood in our Western world, but we must understand it if we are to walk in wholeness, live in His joy, and function as children of God.

First, the Hebrew meaning of *fear* is "to stand in awe before someone of great power, to reverence (to show honor, deep respect, homage, adoration, devotion, worship), respect (regard, esteem, praise, admire) and honor (glorify, exalt, consider great, have regard for, to bow before)."

Secondly, a "name" is not to be understood as an identifying "handle," or appellation by which we call somebody. In the days of the Old Testament, a person's name meant something. It was usually a sentence describing the kind of person the parents wanted their child to become.

A name came to mean the person's character, their track record in life, and their reputation. Whether or not you trusted them, hired them to do a job for you, married them, or lived in their neighborhood, had a lot to do with the meaning of their names. In other words, names represent both character and reputation.

God's name is synonymous with His character. It represents who He is, His reputation in history as it is recorded in the Bible, and His track record in His dealings with mankind. Can we trust Him? Is He faithful regardless of the circumstance?

Countless scriptures extol the faithfulness and trustworthiness of God. The incarnation, life, death, and resurrection of His Son, Jesus Christ, is the supreme illustration of His love for us. Knowing this, we "fear His name." We give Him reverence, honor, and respect, which is expressed through our obedience to Him.

As we walk in the fear of His name, we experience the healing rays of the Spirit of God who lives within our spirit. Over time, we are made into whole people, and our lives are characterized by joy.

> For Thy name's sake, O Lord, pardon my
> iniquity, for it is great.
>
> Psalm 25:11

David says that his only hope for salvation is in the name of the Lord. Though salvation must begin with the deliverance from sin, it means a lot more than that. It also means to come into spiritual, mental, and emotional health. It brings a person from the enslavement to sin into the freedom for which God created and redeemed him in Christ Jesus.

To know the name of the Lord is, therefore, the most important and life-changing knowledge that a person can experience. The entire issue of salvation—spiritual, mental, and emotional health—is a matter of whose name we are trusting.

If we do not know His name or have a confused or distorted understanding of Him, our lives are aimless, pointless, and fruitless. That is why it is vital to have a correct perception of God. Unfortunately, many believers have an incorrect image of Him. When they hear the name "God," their blood turns cold with the wrong kind of fear. Instead of reverence, awe, and gratitude, they cower in terror. That's why we must ask ourselves, "Just what does the name 'God' mean to us?"

# Chapter 2

## The Name of God

Many people fear the name of God in a very negative fashion. Being "terrified" of Him would be a better description. Their fear is the dread and apprehension one gives to a powerful enemy rather than the respect and honor that are given to a dear friend and lover.

Those who grew up with a clear image of a God who loves them limitlessly and unconditionally find it difficult to understand people who are genuinely afraid of Him. However, the people who possess fear-filled resentments of God were raised in homes or sent to schools where discipline found its authority in reminding the children that all bad little boys and girls are sent to hell.

The very mention of the name "God" to such people brings up horrifying images of someone who, if ever He got His hands on them, would do them eternal harm. Yet, we see in Scripture that the name of God is the only hope for peace, joy, and salvation.

## Holy Dread

Mary looked at the crucifix over her bed and bowed her head. "I'm sorry. I am truly sorry for being alive and making You suffer," she cried.

There was nothing more to say. Everything she had done that day had been wrong. Her mother reminded her more than once that she would burn in hell if she did not mend her ways.

The day began in her seventh grade religion class. The teacher, with a look of disgust on her face, had glared at the class as she told them, "God had only one Son; and because you are such vile sinners, that one Son had to die. Just remember that every time you sin!"

Mary later forgot to pick up groceries from the store on the way home from school. Her mother had sent her to her room screaming, "God is a consuming fire! You will burn in hell forever unless you start being a good girl!" She climbed into bed physically trembling and tried to find peace in sleep.

As Mary told me her story, a number of people joined us at the front of the auditorium. I was amazed as they shared their own horror stories of growing up in terror of God. They had good reasons to spend their lives trying to keep their distance from Him!

Their fear caused them to try to please God from the time they were old enough to think. They only did so, however, because they were afraid of Him. They felt as though they never had any hope of gaining His acceptance.

One person said to me, "No one has a hope of pleasing God. He's always mad at us and punishing us for the bad things we've done."

Mary and the others who had gathered around me that night were all believers. As we talked, it became obvious that they were crippled in their relationship with God because of the distorted image they had had of Him since childhood. Unfortunately, this false concept of God had not been repaired when they accepted Jesus as their Lord and Savior.

They shared with me that as adults they had answered a call to be saved because the preacher assured them that saying "the sinner's prayer" would keep them from being dropped into hell when they died. Yet, they were never sure that they had said the right words or expressed the correct feelings of repentance. As a result, they constantly answered similar altar calls on a fairly regular basis.

These Christians hoped that their most recent dedication or cry for salvation would be heard. They desperately wanted to know that they were accepted by God. They often called Christian TV prayer lines. However, they never really believed that God would answer their prayers because they were never quite sure how they stood with Him.

## The Judge

Since then, I have discovered that the little gathering at the front of the church that night expressed the attitude of millions of people who do not have a clear understanding of the name of God. They believe in a cruel and distorted image of Him.

They see God as sovereign, almighty, all seeing, all-knowing, always present, all wise, but first and foremost, the judge of mankind.

The name *judge* colors who He is. He rules the universe to judge it. He is ever present with us, sees everything we do, knows all of our thoughts and desires, and constantly weighs us in the balance. Many believe that His first order of His day is to judge us of our sins. His being the almighty God only means He will get us in the end! We will never be able to escape His vengeance.

Believers who have this image of God do not comprehend that He limitlessly and unconditionally loves them. They cower before Him and are filled with the guilt that they do not measure up. They find it impossible to manufacture any feelings of love for the monster they believe is the God of the Bible.

Furthermore, is not God the Judge? Has He not given us His Law and are we not supposed to keep it? True, God has given us the Ten Commandments, but Satan has distorted that truth into religious lies. The Law has been perverted into the lies from which our pride has willingly fed. These lies have led to our self-hatred and have caused us to shrink before God.

God gave us His Law so that we would get a revelation of how mankind was intended to walk with Him and with each other.

## The Law

The Ten Commandments were the first rays of light that revealed God's love to mankind. These laws also showed us that the universe and the human race have their foundation in the God who is love. Jesus said that the whole Law could be summed up in two sentences.

> ...Thou shalt love the Lord thy God with all thy heart, and with all thy soul, and with all thy mind. And...thou shalt love thy neighbor as thyself.

> Matthew 22:37,39 KJV

Because man was entrenched in selfishness and is antagonistic to the way God is and to the way we were created to be, this revelation had to be delivered in negative terms. The Law was negative to the ears of man because he did not want to love. He wanted to celebrate selfishness!

The Ten Commandments, therefore, became a list of "Thou shalt not's," which Moses brought down the mountain to the waiting people.

The same is true for parental love. When a toddler is determined to ignorantly go his own way, love comes across as a series of negatives. "Don't run across the road!" "Don't touch the stove!" "Don't drink the drain cleaner!"

We must never think of the revelation contained in the Law as a means of salvation. The Law was God's perfect standard, which no person could possibly keep. It pointed to the Messiah, the One who was able to keep the Law. As our representative, we can then receive our pardon and live out the life of love with our Creator through Jesus Christ, the Messiah.

The Law reveals our need for a Savior; it does not save us.

God not only gave us the Law to show us His love and that we were created to walk in that love, but He also wanted to show us how far off we were from the "norm" in which He intended us to live. The Law is the plumb line that shows us just how far away we really are from being whole. It shows us just how much we have rebelled against the character of God and how we have accepted the opposite of God's character as the norm.

When Moses presented the Law to the Israelites, the millions throughout that world who were not present and the billions who were not yet born would by nature be committed to walk in the opposite direction of God's love. Never, at any time in human history, has it been in man's track record to keep the Law out of the innate goodness of his heart! Man's salvation has never been found through his obedience to God.

The Law was given to show us that we are so far off course that we are, in fact, hopelessly lost and only God can save us. The Law drives us to His mercy and grace as we recognize that we are in need of a Savior. Obviously unable to keep God's perfect Law, our only hope is in a Savior who would make it possible for the very essence of our being to be changed.

God's Law might be likened to the mirror in our bathroom. When we look into it, we see how badly we need a shave or a haircut. We do not take the mirror off the wall and try to clean ourselves with it! Once we see what condition we are in, it has done its job and can do nothing more for us. If we continue to look into it, it will only show us more clearly our unkempt condition.

The Law was given to reveal God's character, values, thoughts, and way of living. It then points us to the Messiah, who is the Way, the Truth, and the Life. It reveals the boundaries of protection, provision, and pleasure God has placed around people to give them an abundant, joyful, and peace-filled life. The Law tells us what God's name really means.

Yet, in their total incapacity to perfectly abide by every jot and tittle of the Law, many stand hopeless and helpless, crying out for someone to rescue them from this suffocating predicament. However, instead of embracing the Savior and allowing Him to be Lord of their lives, they see God as the judge and desperately try to find a way to keep His Law.

# Chapter 3

## Keeping the Law

The mirror of the Law drives us away from itself to soap and water, where we will find that which will clean us up. The Law shows us our condition and drives us to God's mercy and grace, which are both found in Christ Jesus.

But mankind was, and still is, so set in his commitment of independence and self-for-self philosophy that the idea of admitting that he is unable to keep the Law is obnoxious to him. He is committed to Satan's lie that he can, and must, achieve perfection independently of God.

> ...you will be like God, knowing good and evil.
>
> Genesis 3:5

Man sets out to be perfect and to be his own god by keeping the rules. In so doing, he will earn acceptance with God and the love and respect of his peers. He not only seeks to keep God's laws, but he also has a list in his head that he believes must be kept in order to be considered the "good" person he is "supposed" to be.

Day after day, people struggle to keep the laws that beckon and call them. At the same time, they shrink back before those same laws, as the mirror continues to accuse and condemn them when they miss the mark. The more they try to achieve their idea of perfection and be what they believe they ought to be, the more they flounder and despise themselves for their inability. They are like a car that is stuck in the mud: The more they accelerate, the deeper they sink.

## A No-Win Situation

This way of thinking causes mankind to define God as the judge who always looks at them with condemnation. We live in terror thinking that He will bring us to judgment and damn us to hell. No wonder so many tremble in their beds!

Our comprehension of being a Christian is of a person who tries to please an impossible God. We carry out our beliefs with resolutions, promises, rededications, and willpower, all of which will sooner or later collapse, leaving us deeper than before in self-hatred and despair.

Neither Mary, nor other believers, came to these conclusions by themselves. For many, this lifestyle was modeled by their parents and was the atmosphere in which they lived. Their concept of the Ultimate Authority in the universe was formed by the example of the temporary authority under which they were raised.

They were brought up in homes where love was earned in one way or another. They had to be a certain type of person and yield to certain demands if they were to receive what they understood to be love. Even then, they knew it was a hopeless task. No matter what they did, love would not be there.

Like Mary, some of us have a one-dimensional image of a wrathful God drummed into our heads. To us, God was always angry, ready to punish and ready to send tragedy into our lives, all because He loved us! In this way, we would be purged of filth and imperfection and be motivated to be good people. But for all the purging we experienced, we knew it was hopeless. There was little doubt that we would end up in hell.

Now, as adults, our relationship with God is performance-oriented: Keep His law, our law, everyone's law and try to be the vague, undefined person we think we "ought" to be. Consequently, our lives are filled with despair and the unending anxiety that we will never be able to attain to the perfection that makes us lovable and acceptable to God or to all of the important people in our lives.

## Sin—Author of Despair

Our despair and frustration are not confined to one compartment of life labeled "religious." If so, we could find relief by shutting that door and walking away. It is what the Bible calls "sin" that poisons every area of our lives. It shows up in how we look at and judge ourselves and others *and* how we believe others must see and judge us.

Listen to how many have shared their hearts with me over the years:

"I always feel guilty about something. I am not what I ought to be, however hard I try. I give up in despair and tell myself that I am not good enough for God or anyone else."

"I am completely unworthy. I can never reach God's standards. No matter how hard I try, I know I will be damned."

"Whenever I finish anything, it doesn't matter what it is, I know it is not as good as it should be. Then, I'm mad at myself for not trying harder. I have to discipline myself to try harder all the time."

"It doesn't matter what I am doing. I always become anxious because I can think of five other things that are more important than what I am currently doing. Many times, I stop doing what I am doing and start doing something else, only to become anxious all over again, thinking that I should be doing the thing that I have just stopped! I can never do anything right."

"The truth is, I hate myself. And I know anyone who knows me must hate me, too! I decided a long time ago that if there is a God in heaven, He must despise me for being no good. I am so far from what I ought to be."

"God is like a giant scorekeeper! He watches all of the bad and stupid things I do and takes notes. One of these days, I am going to wake up and know He has told me to get out of His sight. It's inevitable, and I can't blame Him."

Trying to live by the Law cripples our relationships with others. We constantly chart our progress with them. Self-righteously, we compare ourselves and preen our feathers when we realize that we are not as bad as they are. In a sick kind of way, we enjoy being around those who have broken the Law in a public and scandalous way. In comparison, they make us look like saints.

This way of life also makes us bend over backwards to achieve the affirmation and praise of other people. We look at ourselves through the eyes of others. If they say we are good, we feel elated. If they put us down and point out our faults, we fall apart. We become what and who they say we are.

We believe we should please everyone at all times. Therefore, when we see the slightest hint of displeasure on another person's face, we are filled with self-hatred. We see ourselves through their look of displeasure and believe we are unlikable and even unlovable. We thus despise ourselves.

## Trusting in the Wrong Name

All of these people have one thing in common. They are trying to be saved by trusting in their own name. They are appealing to their own human ability to keep the Law rather than admitting the truth. They have hopelessly fallen short and stand in total need of God's deliverance.

The tragedy is, these people claim to be born again! They live in misery and are dysfunctional because they have not yet recognized that their sins, past, present, and future have been dealt with by God through the work of Jesus on the cross. They do understand that salvation means they are fully accepted by what He has done, not by what they have done.

The misunderstanding of salvation goes something like this: "I now have a clean slate. God has pardoned me, and I am finally in a position to begin again with no past to haunt me. I'll show God that I can keep His Law and be the perfect person I know I ought to be!"

Suddenly, the anxiety, guilt, and self-hatred return in industrial strength intensity as they strive to keep the Law. Soon, they find themselves struggling in the same way they struggled as a nonbeliever! Now it is worse because it is in a religious context. Listen to the believers who are enslaved by the Law:

"Whenever I come before God, I am ashamed I don't have enough faith for anything. I must read the Bible more, confess it all the time, and build my faith."

"I am a total failure at being a Christian! I am not what I ought to be. I should read my Bible more, pray more, and be at church every time the doors are open."

"Nothing has gone right this week. I must search my heart to see if God is punishing me."

"I live in a constant state of anxiety wondering if God will be mad at me if I go to X, if I read Y, or spend time with Z."

Every so often, the poor dysfunctional believer musters all of his willpower: "I hate the way I am! I know God must hate it, too. I am determined to try harder to be what He wants me to be. I will rededicate my life to Jesus and resolve that I am not going to sin anymore."

After the act of resolution, the believer looks and feels great: "I just feel inside that this is it! This time I really mean it! I am dead to self. I am going to live for God for the rest of my life. I am resolved to please Him in everything I do."

Unfortunately, when you meet him at the end of the week, it is the same old story of despair and depression: "I've sinned again. I can't face God. I've let Him down. What's the point of praying or reading the Scripture? It would be hypocritical to pray now. The Bible condemns me even more. I hate myself, and I am certain God must be disgusted with me, too."

Even on their better days, these people grovel in their prayers and whine to God that they are not good enough to receive His mercy. At other times, they grow tired of struggling to be good and decide they need a reward for their religious sweat—a day off to do what they really *want* to do! They always indulge in the wrong pleasures or too much of the legitimate ones. They drown themselves in sex, drugs, alcohol, or food, and then hate themselves as they stand in condemnation before God.

## Pride Brings a Fall

Mark poured out a story filled with the pattern I have just described. At the end, he looked up at me in despair. "I went to my pastor and told him some of this. I was too afraid to tell him everything. He told me to get up early every morning and pray and read my Bible and to attend church more often. I felt as though the bottom dropped out because I have resolved to do that ten times a year for the last five years!"

He sobbed, "What's the matter with me? Why can't I live the Christian life like everyone else? Am I crazy or demon possessed?" He buried his head in his hands, "What's the use? I can't be good enough for God or man. Everyone thinks I am a Christian, but I'm a phony hypocrite."

Jack's story was perhaps more tragic in that he was a minister of a growing church. He shared with me that he despised himself because his congregation did not know who he really was. He saw himself as a phony. "I have a split personality!" he cried. "One part of me loves God and wants to live and serve Him. The other part, which most of the time seems to be my true self, has no desire to seek God at all. There are times when I don't know if I have a real self. I hate myself for being a hypocrite. I am coming to the point where I have nothing more to give anyone. I believe I must quit the ministry in order to be honest with myself and everyone else."

> Humble yourselves, therefore, under the mighty hand of God, that He may exalt you at the proper time, casting all your anxiety upon Him, because He cares for you.
>
> 1 Peter 5:6,7

Ironically, the basic problem these people have is the sin of pride, which is the main ingredient of man's original departure from God in the Garden of Eden. Satan introduced the great lie. He told Adam and Eve that they could be like God if they would declare themselves independent of Him. Instead of humbling themselves under the mighty hand of God and resisting the devil, their response to the devil's lie was pride, and they arrogantly believed the lie.

The rebellious pride of our heart says we can be perfect by fulfilling God's Law. In doing so, however, we function in life without His grace and mercy. We believe that God has to accept us because we have kept His Law and have met His standards.

Our pride doesn't stop there. We add our own laws to God's Law, and our laws are much more demanding than His! We set impossible standards for others as well as ourselves in celebration of what we perceive as our limitless ability to be perfect. Inevitably, our pride is smashed when we do not keep these laws, so we spiral into despair and depression.

There are a few who have the willpower to meet their own standards of excellence and keep the laws that they have set for themselves—at least in their own minds. These poor people are self-deceived and are in worse condition than those who come to the end of themselves. They sincerely believe they do not have need of a savior. If they are believers, they feel they don't need His daily intimacy, grace, or mercy. As a result of this deception, they never notice the slow deterioration of their lives.

## Breaking Away

To completely turn from this cycle of destruction, our first step toward wholeness is to understand the incredible, unconditional, and limitless love that God has for us. The judge Himself is the One who bore the penalty that justice must pronounce over our sin. The name of the Lord, which is our only hope of salvation, is love. Until we fear and reverence that name, and only that name, we cannot be healed.

We need to see that God is love, and it is this predominant attribute of love that enables us to understand all of His other attributes. The One who rules His universe is all-seeing, all-knowing, and limitlessly present to bless us. The ultimate blessing and the beginning of our deliverance from darkness is that Jesus Christ became our sin that we might become righteous. Although slaves to sin and a life of despair, Jesus purchased us and gave us freedom through the shedding of His blood.

As we move into the knowledge of the name of the Lord, we break free from the bondage of

the Law and move into the joy of living a life of
being loved and loving others.

# Chapter 4

## The Price Hosea Paid

In the Old Testament, God demonstrated what the Messiah's sacrificial love would be like through the life of Hosea, one of the ancient prophets of Israel. The Israelites had turned away from God and were seeking to fill their emptiness through every kind of substitute the human mind could invent. God, therefore, decided to speak to them in a way that they would never forget.

He directed Hosea to marry a woman whose name was Gomer. God knew her heart better than she did. He knew that she would not be faithful to Hosea and that she was bent on a path of unfaithfulness and adultery. In the same way that the people of Israel had turned from God to idols, Gomer would turn from her husband to other men.

Hosea knew nothing of God's plan to make him a living illustration of a Messiah whose love is beyond verbal definition. The love of the Savior can only be defined and known through a person. Jesus was a human being just like we are; however, He never sinned. He exemplified the character, actions, emotions, and thought patterns of God. He taught His disciples that if they knew Him, they would also know the Father. (John 14:7.)

In the same way that God revealed Himself to us through His Son, Jesus, He chose to speak to Israel about their Messiah by using Hosea. The life of Hosea brought a three-dimensional, living and breathing image of the Son of God to a people who were terribly lost and who were destroying themselves through sin.

## The Tragic Marriage

Hosea's marriage to Gomer took place in his hometown of Samaria. Because he was a prophet and God's voice to the nation, his marriage was reported for miles around, to the borders of Israel.

We have already discussed the significance of a name in biblical times. When Hosea and Gomer's children were born, their names were short sentences, as was the custom of the day. In each case, their names described the spiritual condition of the people of Israel. Were these names also a reflection of the emerging tragedy of the marriage?

The little child named "No love left" described the breaking of the relationship between God and Israel. This name also foretold the disintegration of Hosea's marriage, as Gomer began to be unfaithful.

The baby they named "Not mine" described Israel as no longer being in God's family. Did it also reflect the painful thoughts of Hosea as he wondered if he was really this child's father?

Hosea's family publicly played out their sadness. Their shame and humiliation were under the watchful eyes of the nation as his wife continually flaunted her unfaithfulness.

Not long after her infidelity began, Gomer abandoned Hosea and her children for her rich paramours, who showered her with gifts and money. These men were the Israelites who had abandoned their faith in God for Baal and Astoreth, pagan deities that dotted the hills and promised wealth in rich harvests. As an act of worship, they demanded that all forms of lust and immorality be performed in their temples.

As time passed, Gomer's lovers became bored with her and left her for new conquests. Left alone on the streets, she did whatever she could to make a living. She began to sell her body in order to make money for bread. It is possible that she also went to the temples of Baal and participated in the degrading acts of worship that took place there. If this is so, she not only flaunted her unfaithfulness to her husband but also to God. She was on the payroll of the demonic Baal spirits, the sworn enemies of the God of Israel.

Gomer became old before her time and was eventually abandoned. She found herself on the streets again, living in cheap hotels and filthy back alleys.

Finally, she sold herself as a slave for the pleasure of her master. She was sold and resold, a shadow of the woman who had been the wife of the man of God. She was an old hag, bent and bitter, living through the pain of one day into the hell of the next. She was no longer news; the scandal had become history. No one knew where she was, and no one cared.

## Love Hits the Streets

Hosea helplessly watched as his life unraveled before him. While the streets of the cities of Israel buzzed with the scandal, Hosea raised his children. God spoke to him and told him to find Gomer, confirm his love for her, and receive her back into his house!

All kinds of questions must have flooded Hosea's mind. Gomer had paraded her unfaithfulness, joined herself to God's enemies, and become the object of ridicule to every decent person. In her current state of degradation and clearly at ease in her moral and physical filth, would she even want to come home? Was there any point in finding her and bringing the sordid affair to public attention once again?

Beyond any other consideration, where could a man find the kind of love it required to embrace the bent frame of such a woman? She reeked of immoral living and her eyes reflected the hate and bitterness buried so deeply within her heart. She had deliberately chosen this way of life and rejected Hosea as her husband.

Nevertheless, as Hosea chose to obey God's command, a supernatural influx of divine love drove him to the streets to find his wife. Searching through the taverns and cheap rooming houses, he finally heard of a slave auction where Gomer was the special of the day.

When he arrived at the auction, the prophet of God searched the crowd. A sea of immorality surrounded him. Then he saw her. His eyes reflecting the unconditional love of God watched as she was brought to the platform for bidding. He never looked at his unfaithful wife based on what she had done but on who he was.

According to the Law of Moses, he could have demanded that Gomer be stoned. However, Hosea's love was nonjudgmental. Like Jesus, he did not come to mock her or to bring public judgment against her. He was not in the milling crowd to condemn her or to condone her sin. He came to save her and bring her into a new life, a life that could only be described as resurrection from the dead.

## The Great Exchange

If she had looked up from her chains to scan the crowd, Gomer would have seen Hosea and believed that he was there to ridicule and throw her unfaithfulness in her face. In her wildest dreams, she could not have imagined a love like his. It probably never crossed her mind that the person she had so deeply wronged was there to buy her out of slavery and restore her as his bride.

To the utter amazement of the crowd and Gomer's complete shock, Hosea placed a bid on her. His asking price was extremely low; it was obvious, however, that no one would bother to outbid him. In terms of coins, it was a mere pittance, the price of a wasted slave. In reality, it cost Hosea everything he had.

When Hosea began to walk toward the platform, he was known to everyone as God's man in

Israel. The crowd parted to let him make his way
to the auction block. In front of those in atten-
dance, he ascended the steps and took the woman
who was first his by marriage and now by
purchase. Gently, he unlocked the chains and
embraced her.

Although he never participated in her sin, he
publicly became identified with Gomer's shame
when he embraced her. In turn, she became identified with Hosea's righteousness even though she
did not deserve it. Then, hand-in-hand, they
walked through the silent crowd and went home.

When Hosea claimed Gomer as his own, he
gave her value. His embrace said that this woman
was worth much more than the few shekels he
paid. The most respected and honored man in
Israel who uniquely represented God to the
nation, proclaimed his love for his wife in the
most vivid and public fashion. He bestowed

honor and worth on her in a way that could only be considered priceless.

Before the gaping crowd, he played out "the great exchange." His public embrace took upon himself Gomer's dishonor. It was swallowed up in his God-ordained love for his wife. The moment he identified with her shame, she became identified with his honor and dignity.

Although Hosea became identified with her sin, he did not become dirtied by it. His worth in the eyes of the Israelites did not lessen when he engulfed her rebellion. At the same time, she was surrounded by his integrity and love and was given a new life.

Hosea and Gomer were one flesh. To despise and attack her now would be the same as despising and attacking him. She was what she was only because of the kind of person he was.

As all of Israel pondered this unfathomable act of mercy and grace, God directed Hosea to use the national scandal to teach them about His unconditional love for mankind. Hosea's story serves to enrich the lives of all believers when they come to an understanding of His marvelous grace and mercy toward them.

# Chapter 5

## Trusting in His Name

The human race as a whole, and as individuals, is very much like Gomer in that both have rejected God's love and have fled from Him. And like Gomer, we have pursued every substitute for His love that we could find. In our search, we have found that without God there is no meaning to life. We have joined the enemy's camp and have become slaves of the very things that promised us freedom.

God, however, has not left us. He came to where we are. He followed us to the streets and pursued us to wherever our missing the mark took us. Jesus took upon Himself our sin; yet, He did not become sinful. He bore our shame and rejection and dealt with it once and for all in His death. In His resurrection, He holds out His nail-scarred hands and bids us, "Be My bride and come to My home."

## There Is No Other

One of the great healing promises of Scripture is in Acts 4:12. Speaking of the name of the Lord Jesus, it says:

> And there is salvation in no one else; for there is no other name under heaven that has been given among men, by which we must be saved.

The expression "no other name" means that the name of Jesus is exclusive. Nobody else has attained to His class. There is no second opinion in the matter—and that includes the possibility of salvation or wholeness through our own name. We are saved by who He is, not by who we are or what we have attained in our past.

Jesus Christ is the final declaration of the name of God. The Father sent Him because He loved the world. He willingly took upon Himself our humanity, and the Creator became the created. He lived out the perfect lifestyle of love and was tempted in every way that we are. However, instead of choosing to sin, He chose to follow after righteousness.

Jesus kept all of the "Thou shalt nots" written in the Law, as well as walked in love toward those around Him. He not only loved His neighbor as

Himself, but He also loved His neighbor *more* than Himself!

The One who lived out His life of love under every circumstance chose to offer Himself as the payment for our sins through His sufferings and death on the cross. He offered His perfect life to the Father to be punished for the sins we committed.

It is because of *who* Jesus is that *what* He did has meaning. He is the man who is God. He lived among us as a man. He was tempted but overcame sin and Satan through the Word of God and by the power of the Holy Spirit. Today, we overcome in the same way.

He lived as our supreme example. His death and resurrection provided mankind with a way back to God. His victory over Satan enables us to live as He lived and do the works that He did. (John 14:12.)

Jesus is God the Creator who, because of His great love for man, became flesh and lived among us. This means that He is simultaneously God and man. He is a man of limitless worth.

God became a man in order to become a substitution for the entire human race. Every one of us was "in" Him. What He did, He did as and for every one of us. He lived His life to not only become a showcase, but to also be our representative and substitute. He overcame Satan in the wilderness for us. His victory is our victory.

Jesus' sufferings encompassed all of the pain and poverty that sin caused. He bore all of our griefs and sorrows. In His death He willingly accepted our punishment for sin. When He was buried, we were buried with Him. As a result, our lives of selfishness and sin are over.

Our sins are now paid for, not in ourselves, but through the God who so loved us that He became our representative and substitute. He laid down the ultimate track record of love throughout history and died for us as a man.

Having paid the penalty for sin, Jesus rose from the dead to be the beginning of a new human race. He is now the source of the life that He demonstrated while on the earth. We once were dead in our rebellion, but He has now enabled us to live a victorious life by accepting what He has done.

## David, Israel's Representative

Jesus' act of love and sacrifice is illustrated in many heroes of the Bible, but one of the most famous is found in 1 Samuel 17. The Philistines had invaded Israel, and a decisive battle was set with the two armies facing each other across a valley.

As was common at that time, the Philistines put forward their champion warrior, an enormous man who towered nine feet. Clothed in his armor, he looked even larger. With a booming voice, he challenged Israel to send out their champion. The battle would be won or lost by the two men who represented their nations.

The idea was that the entire army and nation was bound up in this one person who would represent them. The history of Israel's champion would become the history of every Israelite. If he won, everyone would be part of his victory. If he lost, every person in the nation would go under with his defeat.

For six weeks no one had volunteered from Israel's ranks. They were paralyzed with fear. By this time, the giant came right up to the front lines of the Israelite army and mocked them for their cowardice. The battle was all but over, with the Philistines winning by default. The Israelites were cringing before Goliath and nearly accepted their position as slaves.

Then a shepherd boy named David arrived. He was too young to be drafted into the Israelite army. His father had sent him to see how the battle was going and to bring some home-cooked food to his brothers. David heard the Philistine's challenge and, although mocked by his brothers, accepted the challenge.

When David went over the trenches to meet the giant in the valley, he *was* Israel. In this instance, he not only faced the giant for his nation but *as* them. He swallowed up their cowardice with his faith and obedience to God and marched forward to conquer.

When David stopped to pick up the stones from the brook that ran through the valley, the life of every man in Israel was in his hands. As he danced around Goliath, the men in the trenches held their breath. They vicariously faced their enemy through this substitute. When the stone sank into Goliath's forehead and the giant crashed to the ground, the shout went up from the now triumphant Israelite army, "We won!"

David's life paints more pictures of the life of Jesus Christ than any other Old Testament figure. His encounter with Goliath is one of the most powerful types and shadows of the coming Messiah that we find in the Bible.

## The Name of the Lord

God sent Jesus to free mankind from the slavery of sin and Satan. He became like us in every way except He did not sin. He took our place and delivered us from the bondage of sin. His sinless life was not only lived as His own but also *for* us and *as* us.

When Jesus overcame Satan's temptation in the wilderness, He did so as you and me. His victory was placed on our account! He identified with mankind's grief and sorrows through the scourgings He endured before He died. On the cross at Calvary, Jesus took sin and grief from us and bore them as us. His death represented our dying to self—the area of our being that wanted independence from God, thinking that we could find the meaning of life within ourselves.

After Jesus was resurrected from the dead and sat down at the right hand of God, He enabled us to also step into God's presence. Through the blood of Jesus, we can now fellowship with God. We are not only saved and delivered from sin and its crippling effects, but we are also able to stand in the presence of God, accepted by His love. We are not able to stand upright before God through anything we have done or through the arrogant promises of perfection that we make to Him!

We are not saved through our name but by His Name.

He saved them for the sake of His name.

Psalm 106:8

Help us, O God of our salvation, for the glory of Thy name; and deliver us, and forgive our sins, for Thy name's sake.

Psalm 79:9

Although our iniquities testify against us, 0 Lord, act for Thy name's sake...we are called by Thy name; do not forsake us!

Jeremiah 14:7,9

The name of the Lord is a strong tower;
the righteous runs into it and is safe.

Proverbs 18:10

What Jesus gained for mankind on the cross becomes our experience when we repent and trust in His name. True repentance is deliberately turning from trusting in ourselves; i.e., who we are, our reputation, and our track record. We leave all of this behind and begin trusting in who He is, His reputation, and His work on the cross. We now rest in Him with no hope in ourselves.

Faith means that we call on, or trust in, the name of the Lord Jesus Christ.

Jesus illustrated this in a story in Luke 18 about two men who prayed in the temple. One was an extremely religious Pharisee who fervently prayed every day. Jesus pointed out that he "prayed with himself." (v. 11.) He did this by

66

celebrating all of the goodness that he could find in his own character. He believed that his pious living was assurance of his acceptance with God.

A tax collector stood across the room. He was a rich man whose life was filled with corruption and greed. In a posture of pure helplessness, he knew there was no hope in trusting in his own name. He, therefore, called on the name of the Lord.

Jesus said the Pharisee went home in the same way that he had come, without any acceptance from God. The tax collector, on the other hand, was accepted by God because he trusted in the name of the Lord. (v. 14.)

Tragically, many believers do not have a clear understanding about what it means to call on the name of the Lord. Even when they truly believe that Jesus is their Lord and Savior, they plunge on and try to achieve acceptance in their own name.

They intellectually acknowledge Jesus' lordship but do not embrace Him with their whole being or pursue a daily intimacy with Him.

Jesus summed up the entire Mosaic Law as loving God with all your heart, soul, mind, and strength, and then loving your neighbor as yourself. (Mark 12:29-31.) Loving God with all your heart, soul, mind, and strength is far from a mental, religious exercise. Loving God means that every pore of your being trusts, rests, and abides in Him.

Walking in the Spirit simply carries that truth into every area of our lives—whether we are alone or with our family, socializing with friends, are on the job, or shopping at the mall. Being a Christian is responding with the love of Christ in all situations.

## Trusting in His Name

We live out our life in God as we began, by trusting only in His name and having no trust in ourselves. Our name is forever out of the picture as a hope of salvation, healing, or significance. We are accepted and precious because of what Jesus has done and who He is at this moment, to and in us.

# Chapter 6

## Trusting in His Word

When we become born again, which is the first time we understand and respond to God's love, we may experience great joy. However, we only dimly comprehend what we are responding to. Our human mind and heart do not fully comprehend the love God has for us, or the salvation, healing, and deliverance that comes to us in the name of the Lord Jesus.

It is when we are taught and study the Word of God, and as we apply His truths to our everyday lives—always being sensitive to the Holy Spirit who dwells within us—that we begin to comprehend everything that we have acquired by trusting in His name. Through this process, our hearts are filled with joy.

We begin by trusting in the name of the Lord, and we proceed on the pathway of joy by trusting in the Word of the Lord.

The way to wholeness is living in the daily consciousness that we are loved and accepted in who Jesus is and what He has done. We no longer trust in our own name, our own thinking, and our ignorant, foolish words of the past; but we begin trusting in His name, His thinking, and His Words.

## The Seed of the Sower

Through the parable of the sower in Matthew 13, Jesus explained how believers mature in God's love. The sower sowed his seed on various kinds of soil, and most of the seed perished. The seed that lived and thrived did so because of the quality of the soil in which it was planted.

Jesus later gave a detailed explanation of the parable to His disciples. He likened the seed that was sown to the "word of the kingdom," (v. 19) and the soil represented the condition of our hearts.

The "word of the kingdom" is the Good News of God's love to us in Christ—who He is, what He has done for us, and who we are in Him. When the Word is sown in our hearts, whether or not the seed takes root and grows in our lives depends on the state of the soil of our hearts.

And He spoke many things to them in parables, saying, "Behold, the sower went out to sow; and as he sowed, some seeds fell beside the road, and the birds came and ate them up."

Matthew 13:3,4

The first seeds fell on the side of the path and were immediately seized by Satan. He was able to take the seed because the soil was impenetrable. The seed was not able to even work its way under a layer of dust. In other words, the Word was not even considered!

As we have seen, the natural heart of man is at war with God, and man would prefer to trust in his own name. He makes and attempts to keep endless lists of rules and disciplines in order to produce a behavior that will be good enough for God to accept.

# Trusting in His Word

To the natural man, the "word of the kingdom," or the message that God's love for us is not based on our behavior but on who He is, is not good news! This requires that man renounces his trust in himself and trusts in the name of the God of love and what He has done to achieve our salvation and wholeness. When he rejects the Word, Satan is able to snatch it away before he is able to think about it and begin to see the foolishness of the path he is following.

The Holy Spirit enables you to see and understand the nature of God's love toward you. Your heart is not impenetrable if you heard and receive the Word. It is up to you to say "Yes!" to what the New Testament calls the "obedience of faith." You deliberately turn from trust in your own thinking and abandon yourself to resting in His Word.

And others fell upon the rocky places, where they did not have much soil; and immediately they sprang up, because they had no depth of soil. But when the sun had risen, they were scorched; and because they had no root, they withered away.

Matthew 13:5,6

The second response Jesus indicates is that of the people who, with great joy, receive the Word. They can hardly believe that what they are hearing is true. They dare to believe it and discover for the first time in their lives the joy of the Lord and the peace of God. In fact, they want the whole world to know!

However, when they proclaim their newfound faith to the world, they quickly find out that the world does not want to hear about it—and in some cases, neither do people in church! They suddenly find themselves ostracized by many friends and family for daring to believe and live in the reality of the love of God. They soon begin to wonder if so many people could be wrong.

Added to this initial doubt is their failure to look into the Scripture for themselves. They have only heard what others have told them; they have not asked the Holy Spirit to speak to them directly through His Word. As a result, because they have only heard from man and not from God, they become confused by arguments from those who insist that one's acceptance by God is based on their performance for Him.

Eventually, they give up and return to their religious anxiety, wistfully remembering the fleeting moments when they walked in the love and grace of God and momentarily knew what the New Testament promised. The great joy of their salvation has been scorched because they did not have any root or real revelation of the truth within themselves.

> And others fell among the thorns, and the thorns came up and choked them out.
>
> Matthew 13:7

> ...the worry of the world, and the deceitfulness of riches choke the word, and it becomes unfruitful.
>
> Matthew 13:22

The vast majority of believers today can relate to this category more than the other methods in which the devil steals the Word. They have heard and gladly received the Good News of God's love. Their minds, however, are filled with thorns, which are the "busyness" of living, its worries and its dog-eat-dog philosophy. They allow the pressures of life to divorce them from the consciousness of God's love for them.

The only time they think about the love of God is when they sit for a few moments in a church service. The seed of the Good News, however, never gets a chance to grow and bear fruit. For most of their lives they abide in the smog of this world rather than allow the radiance of God's love to bring them out of darkness.

How do we bring forth the fruit of the love of God in our hearts? We must be sure to have the root of His Word in our lives. We cannot simply hear what someone else says; we have to know for ourselves what God says. Otherwise, we will be like those who are easily swayed by religious opinion and quickly wilt under the heat of persecution.

The "weed seeds" and the "stones" are lies that oppress us by laying down false paths and goals. These lies are the energy behind our behavior and must be confronted and destroyed by the truth of God's Word. The seed can then grow in pure soil, and we can become the whole persons that we were created to be.

The lies that pour through your head at both the conscious and subconscious levels and that insist you must be perfect before God will accept you and be considered lovable to Him or anyone else must be replaced by the truth, which says that you are unconditionally loved by God.

The Word of God must become a part of you. It can no longer be foreign to your true self or an alien intruder to your thought patterns. What God says about you must become the stuff of which your thoughts about God, yourself, and others are made.

When you come to the saving knowledge of the Lord Jesus Christ and begin to fear His name and everything that His name represents, and as you live by the revelation you receive from His Word—which is the truth that sets you free—then your heart can be healed, your soul can become whole, and joy and peace will reign in your life.

Instead of walking around like an empty, religious robot, desperate for the acceptance of God, you will walk hand-in-hand with Jesus, confident of the Father's love.

## The Leap of Faith

Like the parable, the seed has been sown in your heart as you read this book. Roots of the Word must grow deep into your being and transform you to make you whole. For this to happen, you must take the leap of faith and receive the Word of God personally. You must recognize that it is true and apply it to your life.

As you read the Scriptures below, open your heart to the Holy Spirit. Let these paraphrased verses become your prayer; then the joy of the Lord will be yours.

Father, I thank You for the unconditional and limitless love You have bestowed upon me that enables me to become Your child.

1 John 3:1

I give You thanks, Father, that my relationship with You is not based on my loving You enough, but rather in Your loving me and sending Your Son, Jesus, to take my place on the cross and die for me so that He can now live within me by His Spirit.

1 John 4:10

Father, I thank You that You are rich in mercy toward me. You have loved me and will always love me with a great love. With no reference to my behavior, You have made me alive through the death of Jesus Christ and have seated me with Him in heavenly places. This is Your gift to me from the beginning to end, and I thank You for it.

Ephesians 2:4-9

Father, I thank You for the kindness and love You have made known to me in the Lord Jesus. I thank You that You have saved me, not on the basis of my behavior, but on the basis of Your love and mercy. Because of who You are and what You have done, You have saved me through the washing of the rebirth and are presently renewing my life by Your Holy Spirit.

Titus 3:4-7

Lord Jesus Christ, I am now and forever in Your presence, and I thank You for the gift of Your grace and peace. I thank You for causing me to know the love that God has for me and for giving me the Holy Spirit as my closest Friend.

Galatians 1:3; 2 Corinthians 13:14

O Lord, satisfy me in the morning with Your lovingkindness that I may sing for joy and be glad all of my days.

Psalm 90:14

Show me Thy lovingkindness, O Lord.

Psalm 85:7

Read through 1 Corinthians 13, and replace the word "love" with "Jesus," for He is love made flesh. Realize that this is exactly the way He loves you.

This is not an exercise in brainwashing but an opening of your heart to the Holy Spirit so the name of the Lord Jesus may be made known to you. Look to the Holy Spirit to continually make the Word of God alive and to communicate the presence of the Lord Jesus to you.

Take your time with each verse. Pray one Scripture for days until it becomes a prayer on your lips when you wake. You will find that you will subconsciously pray it even while you are busy with other things.

I turn Scripture into prayer all of the time and have prayed one verse until I know its truth has been deeply planted in me heart by the Holy Spirit.

Little children sometimes check themselves every day to see if they have grown. Don't do this with your spiritual life. Just give yourself to continually pray the Scripture, asking the Spirit to open your eyes. Do this as you work around the house, sit at your desk, wait in traffic, or drive down the highway. One day, you will realize that you have moved from the darkness of a guilt-ridden past, with its bondage and misery, to the joy and peace that comes from God through Jesus Christ.

# Prayer of Salvation

God loves you no matter who you are or what your past was like. He gave His one and only Son for you. The Bible tells us, "...whoever believes in him should not perish, but have eternal life" (John 3:16). Jesus laid down His life for mankind. He died, was buried and rose from the grave, so that we could spend eternity with Him in heaven and experience His best while we are living on the earth. If you would like to receive Jesus into your life, say the following prayer aloud and mean it from your heart.

*Heavenly Father, I come to You admitting that I am a sinner. Right now, I choose to turn away from sin, and I ask You to cleanse me of all unrighteousness. I believe that Your Son, Jesus, died on the cross to take away my sins. I also believe that He rose from the dead so that I might be forgiven of my sins and be made righteous through faith in Him. I call on the name of Jesus Christ to be the Savior and Lord of my life. Jesus, I choose to follow You and ask that You fill me with the power of the Holy Spirit. I declare that I am a child of God. I am free from sin and am full of the righteousness of God. I am saved in Jesus' name. Amen.*

If you prayed this prayer to receive Jesus Christ as your Savior for the first time, please contact us on our Web site at **www.harrisonhouse.com** to receive a free book.

Or you may write to us at:
**Harrison House**
P.O. Box 35035
Tulsa, Oklahoma 74153

# About the Author

**Malcolm Smith** was born in London, England, and came to the United States in 1964. While the pastor of a church in Brooklyn, New York, his ministry was radically changed by the revelation that the heart of the gospel was founded in the unconditional love of God and expressed to mankind through Jesus Christ through the Abrahamic covenant. He became involved in the charismatic renewal in the sixties and seventies and was heard throughout the world on radio, TV, and through seminars and retreats. He is currently a bishop in the Community of the Holy Spirit. He and his wife, Nancy, head up the Zoe Community of the Holy Spirit in San Antonio, Texas. He conducts retreats and seminars as well as gives spiritual direction.

To contact Malcolm Smith
please write to:

Malcolm Smith
7986 Mainland Drive
San Antonio, TX 78250

Or visit him on the Web at:
www.malcolmsmith.org

*Please include your prayer requests
and comments when you write.*

# Other books by Malcolm Smith

*Let God Love You*

*Never Lonely Again*

*Forgiveness*

*The Lost Secret of the New Covenant*

Additional copies of this book
are available from your local bookstore.

If this book has been a blessing to you
or if you would like to see more of the
Harrison House product line,
please visit us on our Web site at
**www.harrisonhouse.com**

**HARRISON HOUSE**
Tulsa, Oklahoma 74153

# The Harrison House Vision

Proclaiming the truth and the power

Of the Gospel of Jesus Christ

With excellence;

Challenging Christians to

Live victoriously,

Grow spiritually,

Know God intimately.